Francis Torond, c.1785: a fine 'conversation piece' painted on thick laid paper. The draped curtain and elaborate bouquets are typical but, strangely, the chair on the right appears to have no front legs!

SILHOUETTES

Kevin McSwiggan

Shire Publications Ltd

CONTENTS

Published in 1997 by Shire Publications Ltd, Cromwell House, Church Street, Princes Risborough, Buckinghamshire HP27 9AA, UK. Copyright © 1997 by Kevin McSwiggan. First published 1997. Shire Album 335. ISBN 0 7478 0359 5.

Kevin McSwiggan is hereby identified as the author of this work in accordance with Section 77 of the Copyright, Designs and Patents Act 1988.

Printed in Great Britain by CIT Printing Services, Press Buildings, Merlins Bridge, Haverfordwest, Pembrokeshire SA61 1XF.

British Library Cataloguing in Publication Data: McSwiggan, Kevin. Silhouettes. – (Shire album; 335) 1. Silhouettes 2. Silhouettes – History 3. Silhouettes – Collectors and collecting I. Title 741.7 ISBN 0 7478 0359 5

Cover: (Centre) Painted silhouettes of unknown sitters by William Phelps, c.1788, cut out on card and stuck to plaster, with hammered brass frames. (Top left) Silhouette of an unknown lady by Mrs Isabella Beetham, c.1789 (see page 11). (Top right) Silhouette by Charles Buncombe, c.1818-20, of an officer of the 89th Regiment (Royal Irish Rangers), painted on paper, in a gilt wood frame (see page 19). (Bottom) High Street, Newport, Isle of Wight, 1830, showing the lodgings, left, of the silhouettist Charles Buncombe (see page 20).

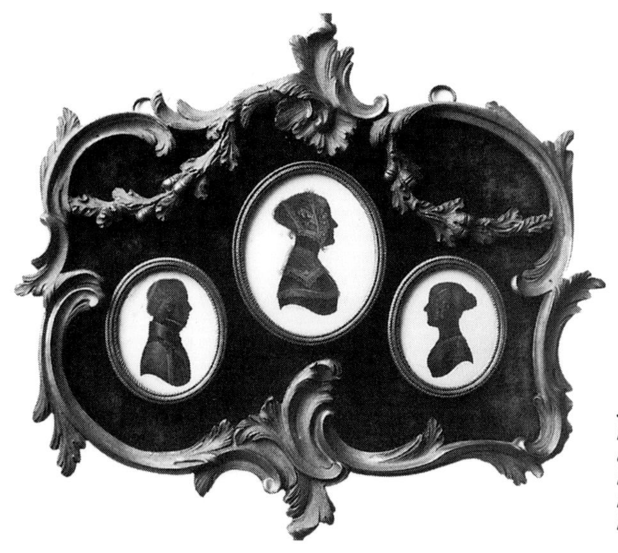

John Field, c.1835: an unknown family group. Silhouettes painted on card and bronzed. The ormolu frame backed in velvet may have been made by William Miers.

INTRODUCTION

It is easy to be drawn into the enigmatic and shadowy world of silhouettes. At their best these 'black shades', as they were originally called, are works of art of real aesthetic merit. At their most modest, they are charming manifestations of vernacular craft. All silhouettes are interesting social documents offering a valuable insight into the past.

To the connoisseur, professionally painted silhouettes are to be coveted because of their wondrous artistry. John Miers's portrait of Nelson (who was quite a skilled silhouettist himself) has an immediacy and presence that is lacking in the more familiar images painted by Lemuel Abbot and Sir William Beechey. The same artist's ravishing portrait of Jane Austen's sister, Cassandra, combines beauty and intrinsic interest as it is the only existing portrait of her as a young woman.

To the historian, many silhouettes cut by amateurs have great historical interest. The Dean and Chapter of Winchester Cathedral own a self-portrait cut by Jane Austen herself, an unflattering matter-of-fact portrayal taken in the last years of her life. George III's six daughters were probably the archetypal Georgian amateurs. Like many leisured ladies of the period, they made intimate silhouette studies of their family as well as all manner of cut-out cupids, animals and landscapes to be stuck into albums along with treasured scraps, theatre tickets and fading flowers.

Gradually, during the nineteenth century, the art of silhouette cutting lost its professional gloss, passing from the fashionable artist's studio to booths at fairs and on street corners. There was one of these booths in the Thames Tunnel, which was a great tourist attraction after its opening in 1843, and several on the Chain Pier at Brighton. Early historians of silhouettes, writing at the beginning of the twentieth century, tended to dismiss most of these later silhouettes out of hand, but modern collectors can now appreciate their unassuming simplicity.

The first historian to attempt a comprehensive listing of silhouette artists was Mrs E. Nevill Jackson in *The History of Silhouettes*, published in 1911, where about seventy-five artists are recorded. Since then scholarly collectors such as Arthur Mayne, Jack Pollak and Peggy Hickman have added to the pool of knowledge. It was left to Sue McKechnie to write the definitive work on the subject, *British Silhouette Artists and Their Work 1760-1860* (1978), which catalogues nearly four hundred artists and has established the standard numbering of 'trade labels' that is universally used by historians, collectors, auctioneers and dealers and is also followed in the present book.

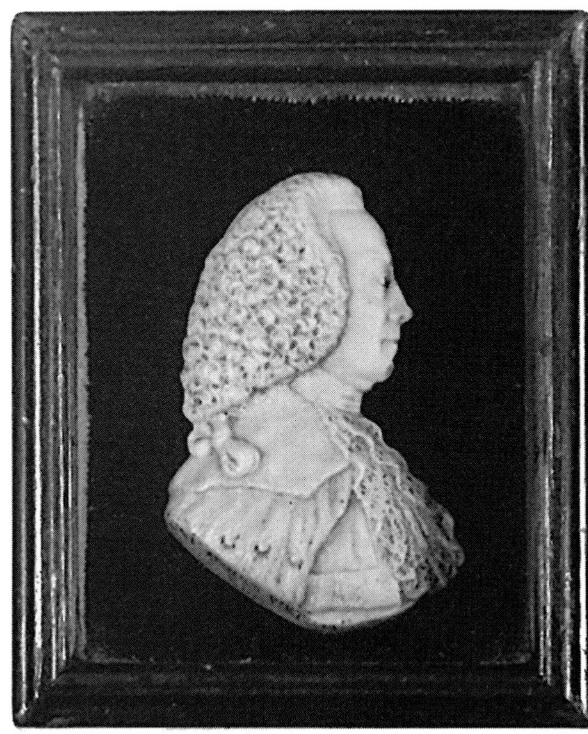

James Tassie, 1779: William Murray, first Earl of Mansfield. White paste, inscribed on the truncation 'Uni aequus virtuti'. Different types of profiles featured prominently in the neo-classical revival. A very similar Wedgwood cameo of the Earl may be seen at Kenwood House, Hampstead, London.

THE HISTORY OF SILHOUETTES

The earliest recorded black shade is a portrait of William III and Queen Mary cut by a Mrs Pyburg in 1699. We owe the name 'silhouette' to Etienne de Silhouette (1709-67), the notoriously tight-fisted French minister of finance. The minister did not invent the process of cutting black paper but simply indulged in the craze of the day; he is said to have covered the walls of several rooms in his château with cut-out portraits. In France this type of art gradually became known as *portraits à la silhouette*, a term synonymous with meanness and parsimony.

In some ways the silhouette may be considered as the 'poor man's miniature' or, perhaps, the forerunner of cheap forms of portraiture such as the daguerreotype. However, it might be argued that the silhouette has its own particular place in European cultural history. On a subjective level, silhouettes obviously had a tremendous sentimental appeal for the sitters and their loved ones, but they were also a product of eighteenth-century aesthetic and scientific ideas.

From an art-historical perspective, silhouettes were a by-product of the neo-classical revival of the third quarter of the eighteenth century inspired by archaeological excavations at Paestum and Pompeii. This was manifested by a rejection of the decorative forms of the rococo in favour of a Greek purity of line: classical profiles are common motifs in the designs of Robert Adam, the medallions of Josiah Wedgwood and the cameos of James Tassie. There was also a vogue for paintings that depicted what was considered to be the birth of painting in Greek times, featuring the 'Maid of Corinth', and modern versions of this legend. De-

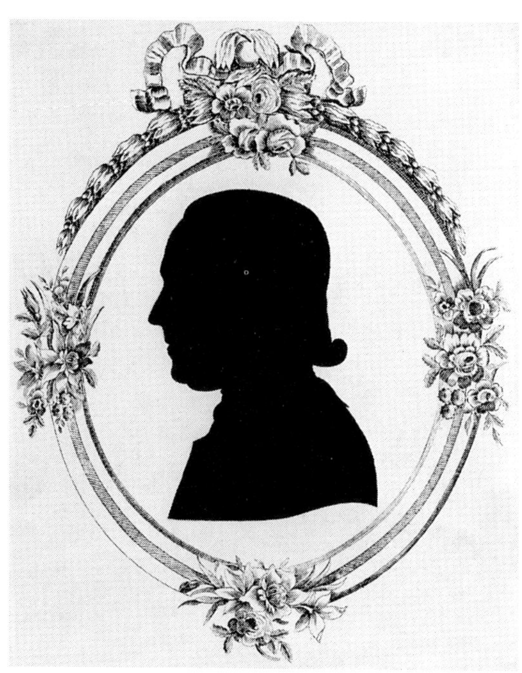

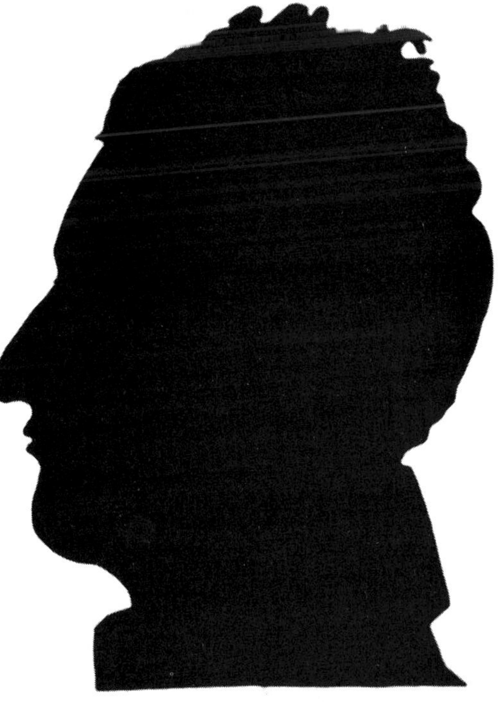

pictions of the maid tracing a silhouette of her lover on a wall may be
found painted by Le Brun, Scheman,
West, Allan and, slightly later,
Mulready. These paintings effectively
demonstrated that the tracing of silhouettes was sanctioned by Greek ori-
gin and was therefore worthy of the
attention of an audience that aspired
to classical literacy.

If neo-classicism shaped the outward
form of silhouettes, their meaning was
influenced by the scientific thinking
of the 'Age of Reason'. At the beginning of the eighteenth century there
was a vogue for physiognomy, the art
of discerning the character of the mind
from the features of the face. For ex-
ample, John Dryden observed that:
'The end of portraits consists of expressing the true temper of those per-
sons which it represents, and to make
known their *physiognomy*.' The Swiss
theologian and poet Johann Kaspar
Lavater attempted to elevate physiognomy to the level of a science in a
treatise of 1775 entitled *Physio-
gnomische Fragmente*, which became a

bestseller in Britain after being translated in 1793 by Thomas Holcroft. Lavater wrote: 'Each perfect portrait is an important painting since it displays the human mind with the peculiarities of personal character. In such we contemplate a being whose understanding, inclinations, sensations, passions, good and bad qualities of mind and heart are mingled in a manner peculiar to itself.' Lavater used silhouettes throughout his book to illustrate his theories, the element of abstraction, in his view, helping to clarify his concepts. The poet Goethe was much taken with Lavater and his silhouettes but turned against him in later life: having decided that a group depiction of his family was unseemly, he ordered it to be destroyed.

Lavater laid out the basic mechanical procedure for taking silhouette portraits in his treatise, and the process came to be known as 'Shadowgraphy'. A patent chair was used in order to hold the subject absolutely still while his or her profile was traced. A candle cast a shadow on to a sheet of tracing paper which was placed behind a vertical glass. The artist simply traced the profile life-size on to the paper: this only required a modicum of practice. Next, the full-sized profile was reduced, using a pantograph (also known as the 'singe', 'monkey' or 'stork's beak'), to the requisite miniature size. The silhouettes were cut, two at a time, and blackened using black paint, Indian or Chinese ink. One silhouette was then framed and a

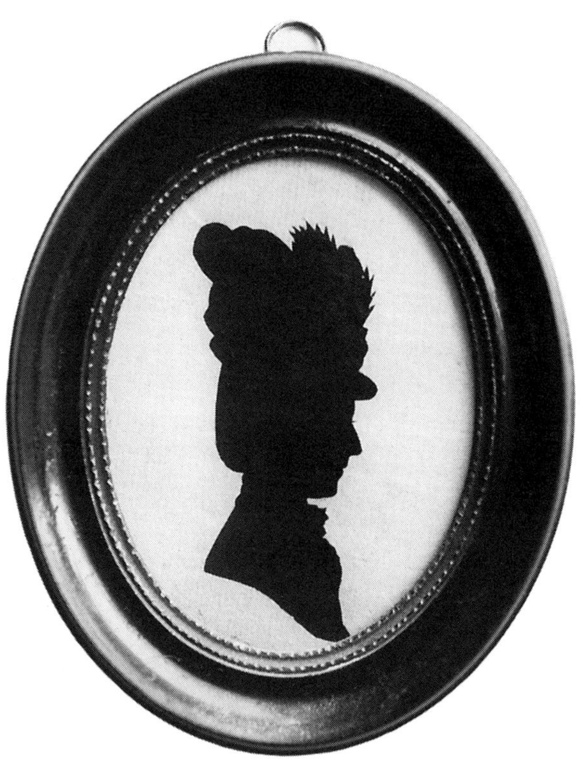

Mrs Sarah Harrington, c.1777: an unknown lady. Hollow-cut silhouette. Ebonised pearwood frame with crenellated gilt surround.

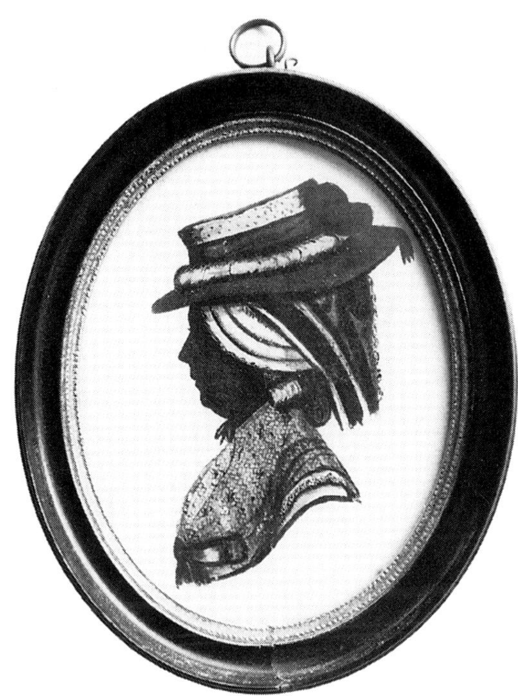

Mrs M. Lane Kelfe, 1784: an unknown lady. Silhouette painted on paper. Inscribed verso: 'M. Lane Kelfe fecit Bath 1784'. Turned pearwood frame.

replica was stuck into the family album.

As the craze took hold, various treatises written in Germany developed the themes of cutting, framing, duplicating and even the home-made printing of silhouettes. The use of the pantograph was extensively described, although it was scarcely a new invention, its origins dating back to the seventeenth century. Rather disingenuously, the English silhouettist Sarah Harrington applied for a patent of the pantograph in 1775, describing it as 'a new and curious method of taking and reducing shadows, with appendages and apparatus never before known or used in the above art'. Early treatises laid great stress on the necessity of obtaining large sheets of paper in order to accommodate the enormous hairstyles of the ladies of the day. Full-sized profiles, which have not been reduced by means of the pantograph, do still survive today, but they are very rare compared to 'cabinet'-sized silhouettes.

Once the vogue for the cut-out silhouette had been established it was reinterpreted throughout the late eighteenth-century decorative arts: Meissen produced elaborate gift sets and souvenir pieces depicting the Elector Friedrich III; Dr Wall at Worcester and other British factories decorated their porcelain with the black profiles of George III and Queen Charlotte. Publishers of biographies commonly used copperplate-printed silhouette profiles of their subjects on the frontispieces of books to demonstrate their subjects' physiognomic probity.

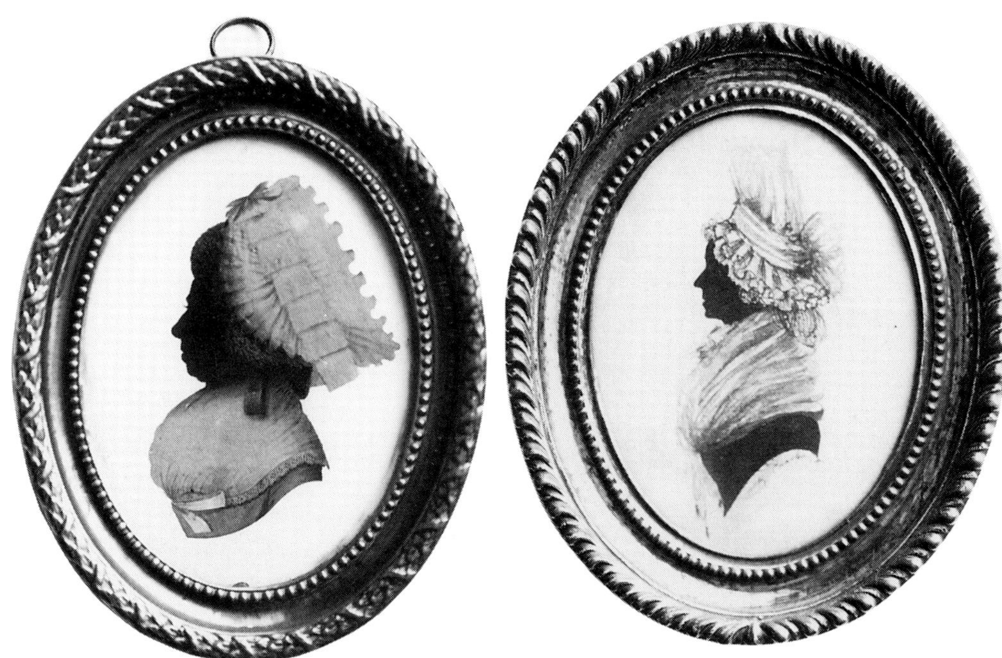

Above left: W. Phelps, c.1785: an unknown lady. Silhouette painted on paper (stuck on plaster) with the sitter's face in black and the dress in lime green. Stamped brass frame.

Above right: A. Charles, c.1788: an unknown lady. Silhouette painted on paper. Inscribed obverse: 'by Charles'. Trade label verso. Stamped brass frame.

GEORGIAN 'BLACK SHADES'

Most cities and large towns in Britain supported several silhouettists during the late eighteenth and early nineteenth centuries. Naturally they tended to congregate in the most populous and fashionable areas. In London, the Strand and neighbouring streets supported a thriving community of mutually dependent miniaturists, jewellers and silhouettists. Amongst these last, the three best-known are John Miers, John Field and Isabella Beetham, but A. Charles and William Phelps also produced fine work.

John Miers (1756-1821) is undoubtedly the most famous silhouettist in the history of the art and his work demonstrates an unrivalled technical virtuosity and flair for capturing a likeness. Miers came originally from Leeds and the phrase 'late of

Leeds' is to be found on most of the trade labels pasted to the back of his silhouettes. In the absence of exhibiting academies and societies for silhouettists, trade labels were an important means of gaining publicity for the artist, providing addresses, technical details of the work, prices charged, etc. They now provide the basic data for historians and prove invaluable when it comes to attribution, authentication and dating. Miers's earliest 'Leeds' labels are rare, for after touring Britain he opened a studio at 62 The Strand, opposite the Exeter Exchange, in 1788.

The secret of Miers's success lay in his technical innovation; he was responsible for perfecting the art of painting silhouettes on very smooth slabs of white

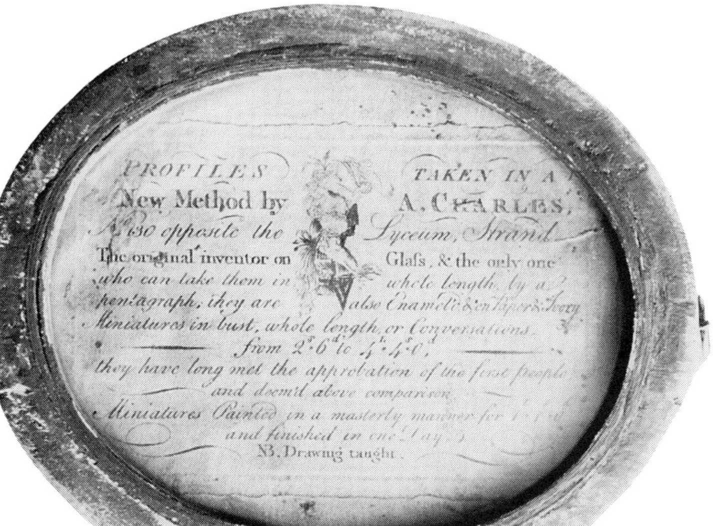

Below: John Miers: trade label number 5.

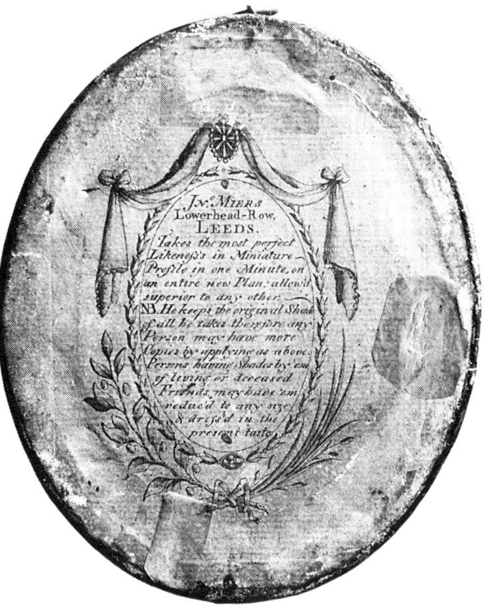

Above: John Miers, c.1784: an unknown gentleman. Silhouette painted on plaster. Trade label number 5. Composition frame. The double concavity of the bust-line termination is typical of the artist's early work in Leeds. Note the turned-up 'Ramillies pleat' and 'fantail' hat of the period.

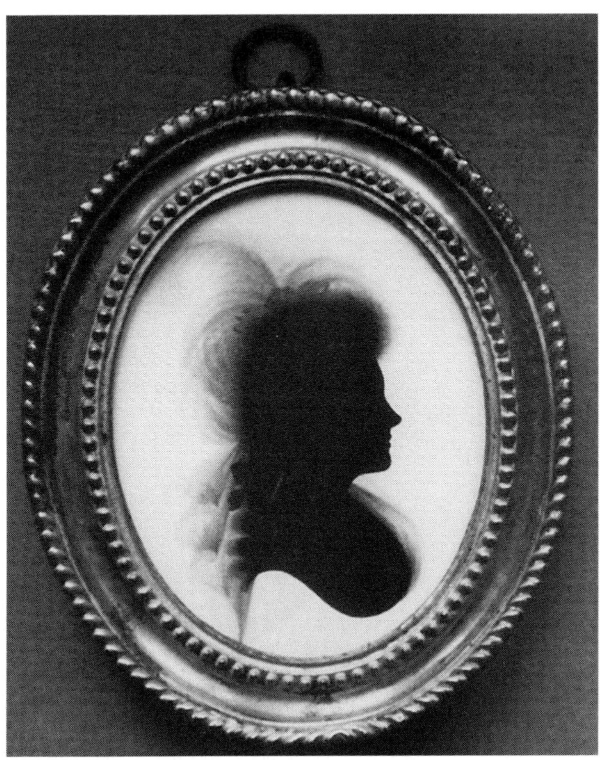

plaster that had been prepared by casting on to sheets of glass. In order to prevent the pigment sinking into the porous surface, Miers used a special medium of pine soot mixed with beer. The result was that he was able to achieve a tremendous subtlety in the gradation of tone, leading to wonderful smoky transparent effects in the elaborate clothes and hairstyles of his sitters. Some writers have termed Miers the 'Cosway' of silhouettists. There are parallels with the famous miniaturist: both artists were able to use their technical gifts to flatter their sitters whilst maintaining an accurate likeness, and both achieved marked success amongst the fashionable élite of society. Various other artists went on to copy Miers's technique and establish what might be termed a 'school of Miers'; these would include Mrs Lightfoot of Liverpool, J. Thomason of Dublin, John Smith of Edinburgh and

Samuel Houghton, who formed a partnership with George Bruce, also in Edinburgh.

A five-minute walk from Miers's studio was that of Isabella Beetham (c.1753-1825) at 27 Fleet Street. Mrs Beetham painted some of the most beautiful of all Georgian silhouettes. Early in her career she cut silhouettes or painted them on plaster or ivory, but she is best-known for those painted on the reverse of convex glass. These silhouettes are usually bust-length, confidently drawn in an enamel-like paint. This sticky paint enabled the artist to dab with her fingertips to produce a hatching effect as a background for the basic elements of the dress, and these fingerprints are often clearly visible in the finished work. This semi-transparent technique was well suited to rendering the texture of gauze and muslin, which were the fashions of the day. With many

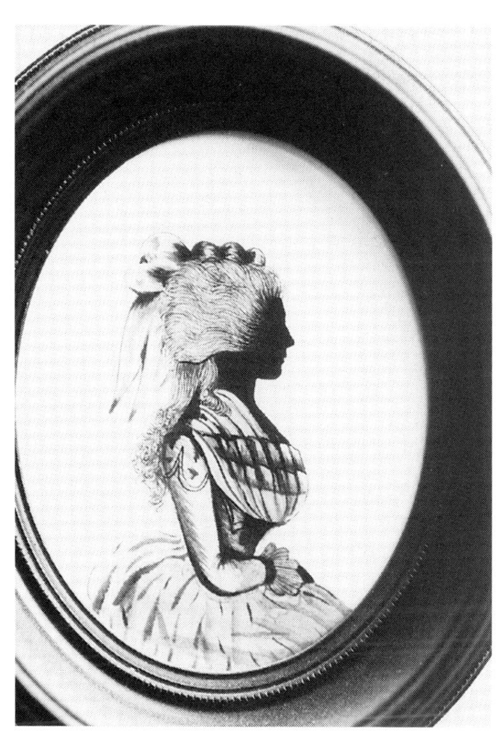

Left: Mrs Isabella Beetham, c.1789: an unknown lady. Silhouette painted on card. Trade label number 5. Turned pearwood frame.

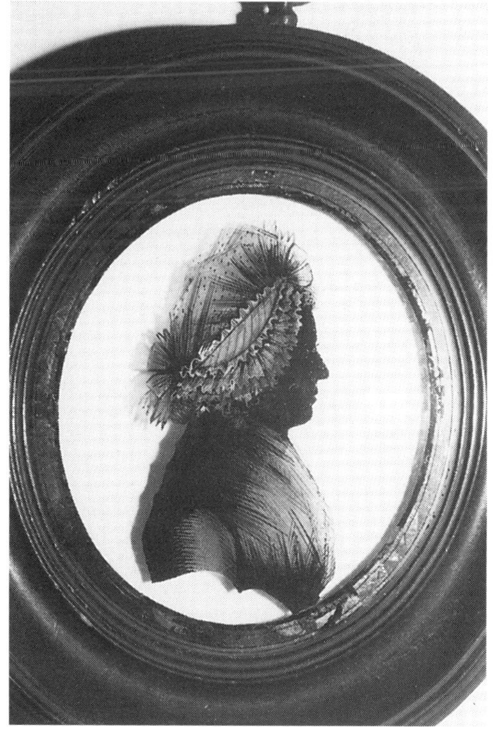

Right: Mrs Isabella Beetham, c.1790: Faith Gray. Silhouette painted on the reverse of convex glass. Trade label number 5. Turned pearwood frame. Note the 'Dormeuse' or French nightcap fashionable in the 1770s.

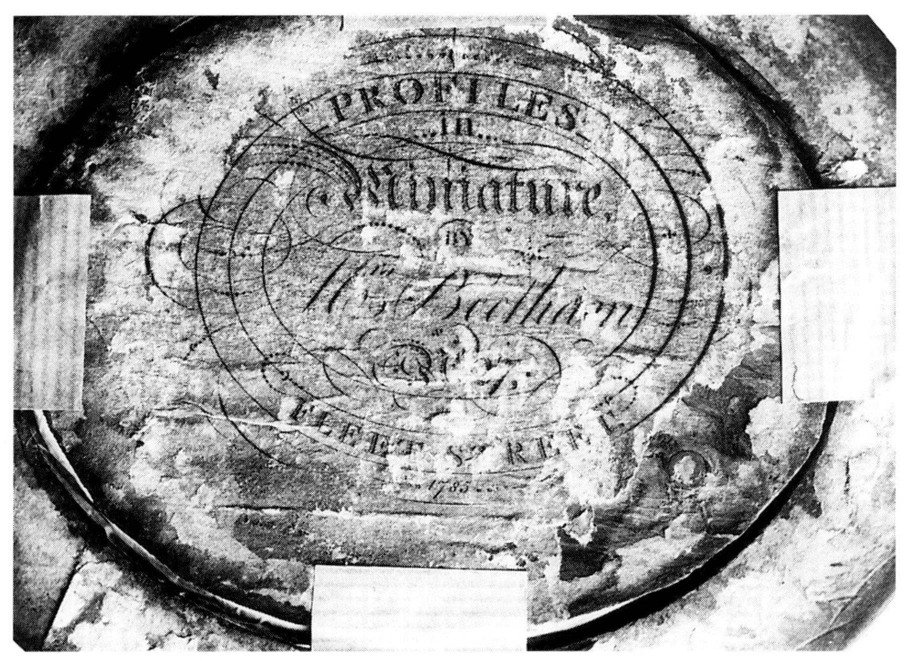

Mrs Isabella Beetham: trade label number 5.

silhouettists, the shape of the bust-line termination is characteristic and is a useful guide to attribution when written evidence is lacking. Mrs Beetham often used a wavy bust-line termination with a pronounced cusp in the middle.

The effects achieved by John Miers and Isabella Beetham make an interesting contrast. In Miers's work the brushwork was of primary importance, whilst in Mrs Beetham's the effect of the whole was given added subtlety by the casting of a shadow from the convex glass on to a flat card or plaster background. These early silhouettes by Mrs Beetham have a particular beauty, but in later years she sought to give the painting more durability by laying down a yellowish wax backing to the paint. These wax backings have suffered from variations in temperature and as a consequence are often to be seen cracking and flaking. The tradition of hanging silhouettes on the chimney wall either side of the fireplace has led to worse problems when the wax has actually melted. On some silhouettes by Mrs Beetham one sees particularly fine *verre églomisé* borders: that is, decorative gold-leaf patterning and painting applied to the back of the glass, which was probably added by the artist's husband, Edward, who learnt the technique in Venice.

In order to run a large studio, John Miers had needed to employ assistants. One of them, John Field (1772-1848), was particularly important, executing most of the studio's output after about 1791. Field fully assimilated Miers's technique but added a new dimension. Using powdered gold mixed with gum arabic, he painted the 'bronzed' detail that is so characteristic of the studio's later production. John Miers's son, William, was a master frame-maker and provided the beautifully cast acanthus-pattern hangers and milled bezels for the papier-mâché surrounds. Working in ormolu, gold and pinchbeck, William Miers also made settings for the

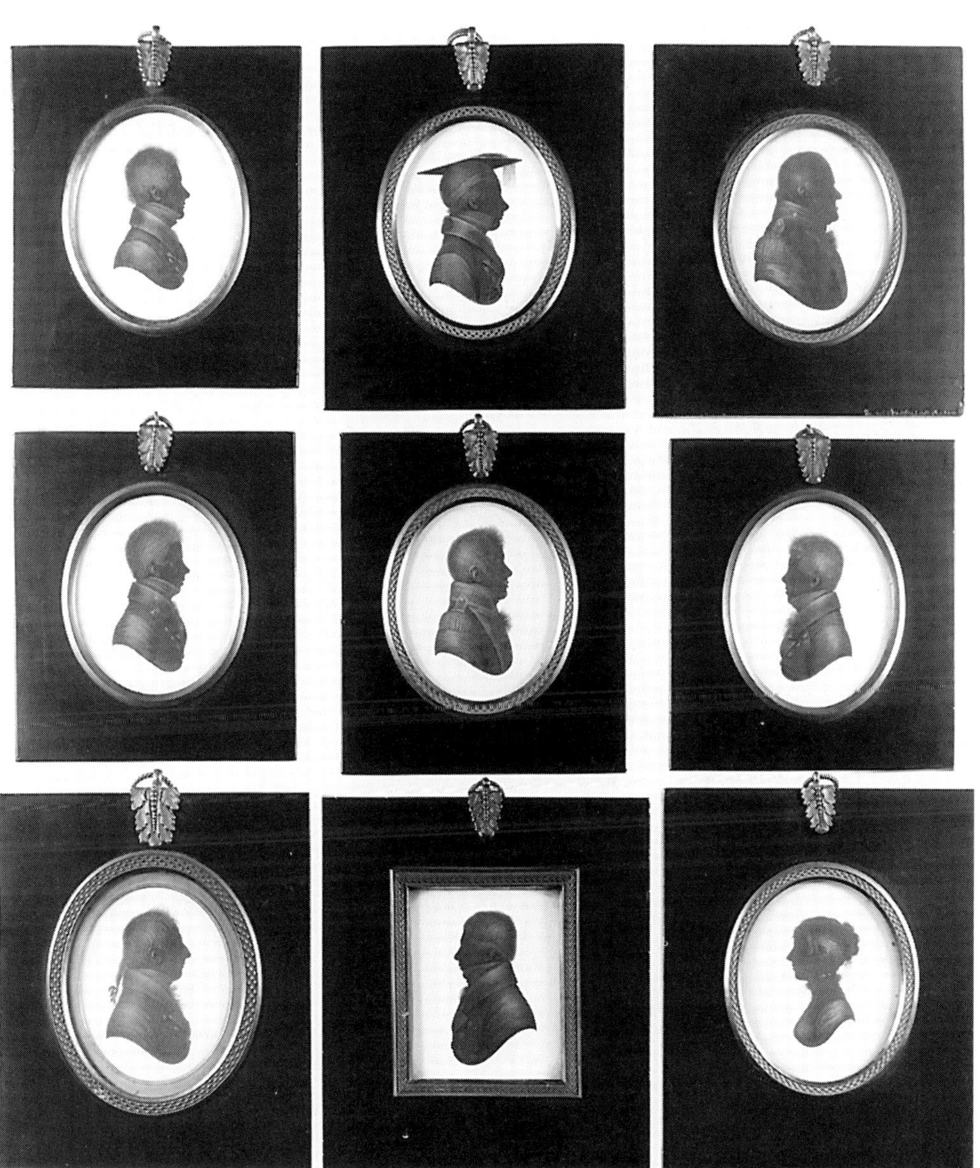

John Field, c.1810-23 (except top right, which may be by John Miers himself): silhouettes painted on plaster. Trade labels numbers (top row from left) 1, 1, 11, and the rest number 12. John Field was a master of the 'bronzing' effects achieved by mixing gold dust with gum arabic. John Miers's son, William, cast the elaborate ormolu acanthus 'hangers' and bezels.

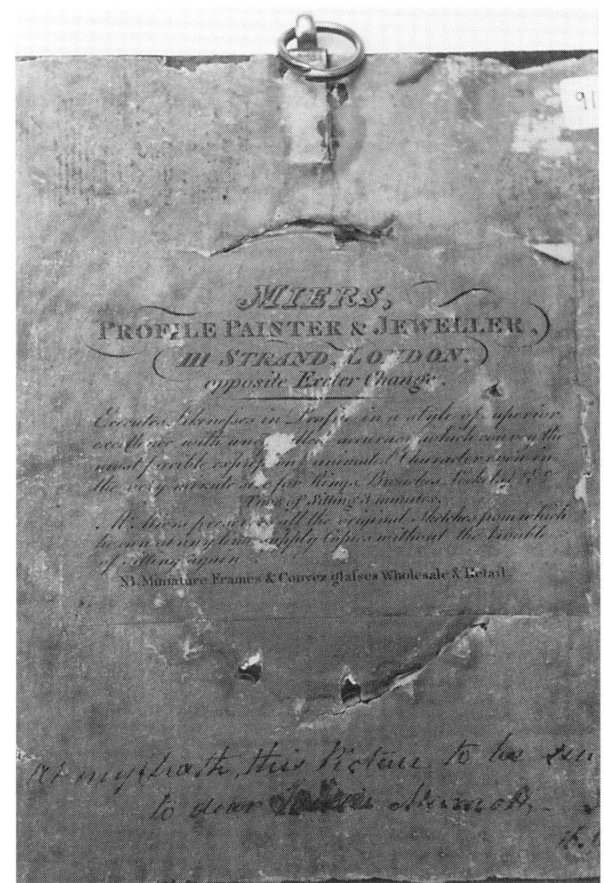

Left: John Miers: trade label number 12 .

Below: John Field, c.1810: an unknown lady. Silhouette painted on ivory in a gold locket, with glazed hairwork.

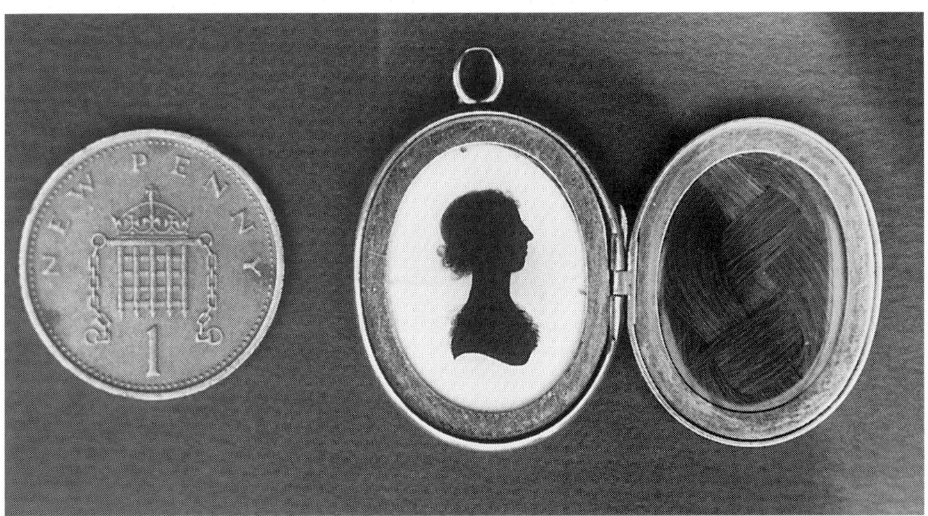

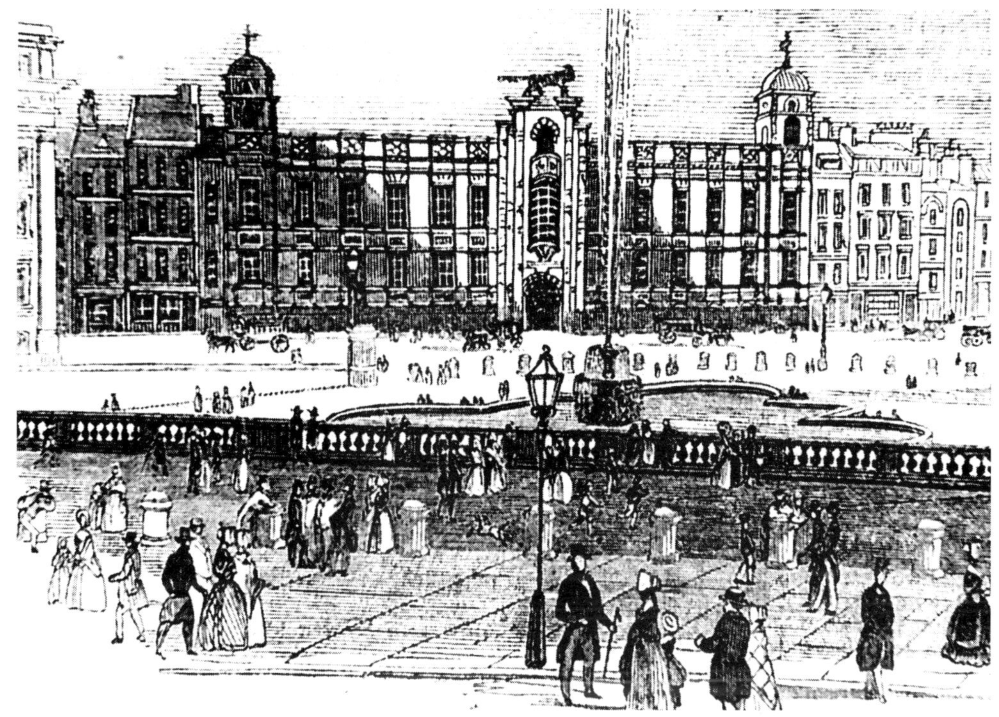

Northumberland House, Trafalgar Square, London, 1845. John Field's house at number 2 The Strand, since demolished, can be seen on the extreme left of the engraving.

tiny silhouettes painted by his father and John Field on ivory for rings, brooches and pins. After the death of his father, William went into partnership with John Field. This partnership was eventually dissolved and Field continued to take silhouettes from number 2 The Strand, close to what was then Northumberland House, where he died in 1848.

A day's coach ride away from London was Bath, the most fashionable spa in the land and the magnet for 'Every upstart of fortune, harnessed in the trappings of the mode', according to Tobias Smollett writing in his novel *Humphrey Clinker* in 1771. Bath was a centre for all types of portrait painting. Amongst many others, Thomas Gainsborough and Joseph Wright painted oils; William Hoare, pastels; Abraham Daniel painted miniatures and

Charles Rosenberg, Jacob Spornberg and William Hamlet painted silhouettes. Artists with studios in the fashionable thoroughfares had to make the most of the bustling Bath season, for later in the year, again according to Smollett, 'Not a soul is seen... but a few broken-winded parsons, waddling like so many crows along the North Parade'.

Charles Rosenberg (1745-1844) came to England in the entourage of Queen Charlotte when she arrived to marry George III. He is mentioned in most of the historical literature on silhouettes and is of especial interest because of his portrayals of the royal family and their court. Many of Rosenberg's sitters are carefully depicted wearing the breast star of the Order of the Garter, and his trade labels and press advertisements vaunt his royal

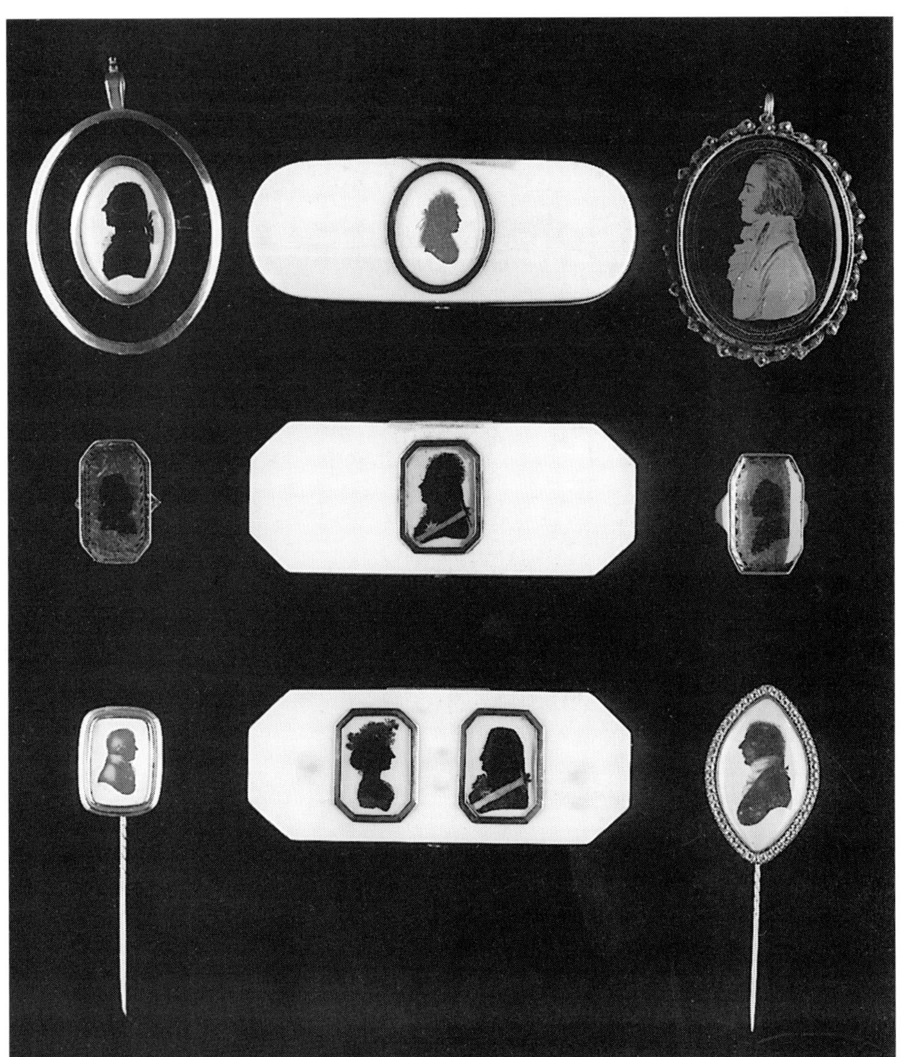

(Top left) Charles Rosenberg, c.1793: a double-sided silhouette of a gentleman and lady. (Top centre) John Miers, c.1795: silhouette painted on plaster mounted in an ivory tooth-pick box. (Top right) Jacob Spornberg, c.1800: 'Etruscan' silhouette signed 'Mr Spornberg fecit Bath' in a marcasite frame with paste border. (Centre left and right) School of Forberger, late eighteenth century: silhouettes painted on gold-coloured glass with 'verre églomisé' borders in octagonal rings. (Centre) Charles Rosenberg, c.1830: King William IV, in coat, order and blue sash of the Order of the Garter. Painted on flat glass against ivory, set in the lid of an oblong ivory toothpick box. (Bottom left) John Field, c.1812: an unknown gentleman. Painted on ivory, mounted as a stickpin. (Bottom centre) Charles Rosenberg, c.1805: Mrs Jordan and the Duke of Clarence, she in dress and veil, he in coat, with badge and sash of the Order of the Garter. Painted on flat glass against ivory set on an oblong ivory toothpick box. (Bottom right) English school, c.1790: an unknown gentleman. Painted on ivory with paste border, mounted as a stickpin.

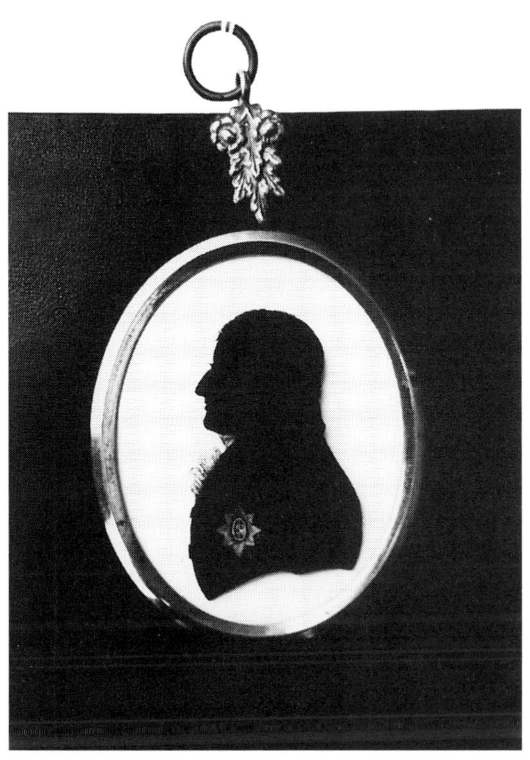

Below: A previously unrecorded trade label of Charles Rosenberg from the silhouette above, c.1805. This is the eleventh Rosenberg label to be recorded. Note the Prince of Wales's feathers, which do not feature on any of the other known labels.

patronage. Most of these silhouettes are painted in dense black on the reverse of convex glass with the details scratched out by a needle. The bust-line termination is characteristic, with a straight cut through the arm and a cusp at the front.

The Etruscan revival was a slightly 'prettified' offshoot of the neo-classical revival proper: Josiah Wedgwood produced 'Etruscan' pottery, James Wyatt designed 'Etruscan' interiors and Jacob Spornberg (1768 to after 1840) painted silhouettes in what he called the 'Etruscan manner'. Spornberg was Finnish by birth but spent most of his working life in Bath. His silhouettes are immediately recognisable by their stunning orange on black palette. Spornberg's technique consisted of painting the design of the silhouette in black on the back of the glass and then applying a coat of orange paint to the

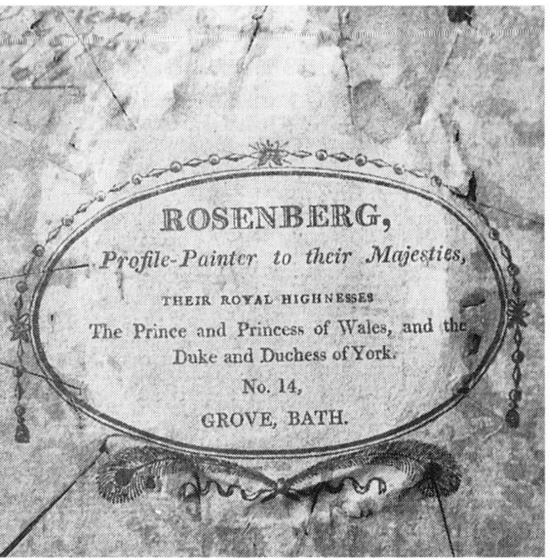

entire reverse surface. This idea was subsequently pirated by Spornberg's rival, Rosenberg, who painted a number of 'Anti-Etruscan' silhouettes in black

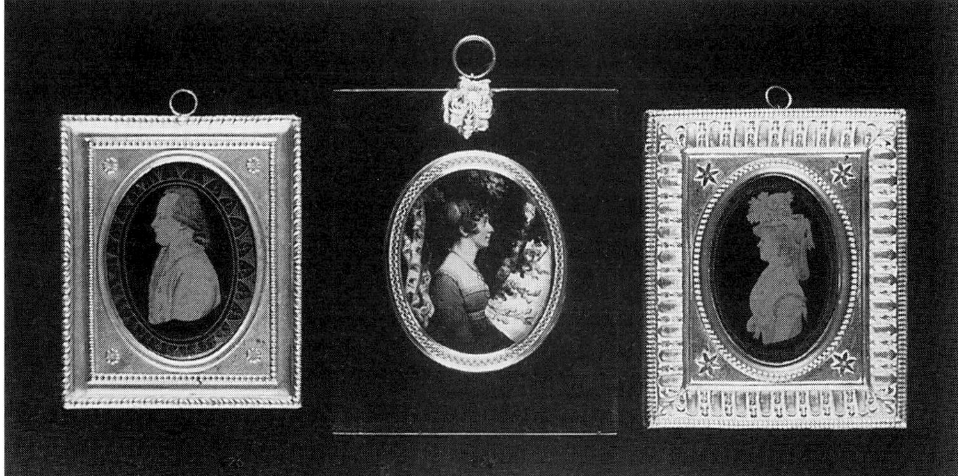

Above: (Left) Jacob Spornberg, c.1790: an unknown gentleman. Silhouette painted in the 'Etruscan manner' on glass. Signed obverse. Rectangular hammered brass frame. (Centre) Mrs Jane Read, c.1810: an unknown lady. Silhouette painted on the reverse of convex glass. Papier-mâché frame. Jane Read was a very sophisticated artist and was the daughter of Isabella Beetham. (Right) Jacob Spornberg, 1773: an unknown lady. Silhouette painted in the 'Etruscan manner' on glass. Signed obverse. Rectangular hammered brass frame.

Below left: William Hamlet the Elder, c.1805: an unknown lady. Silhouette painted on card. Handwritten trade label number 1d. Turned pearwood frame.

Below right: Handwritten trade label number 1d of William Hamlet the Elder.

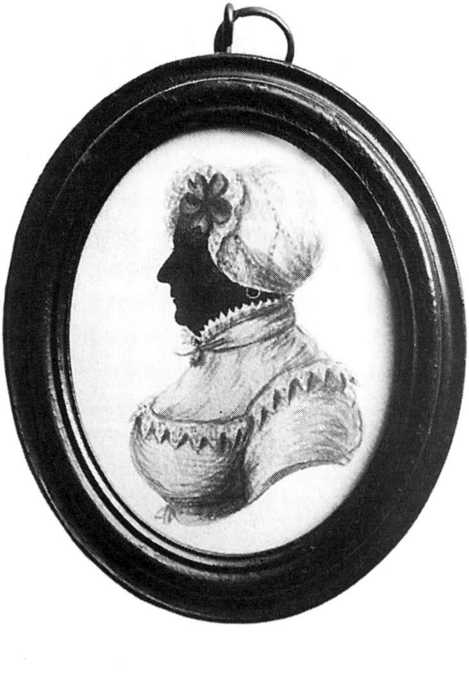

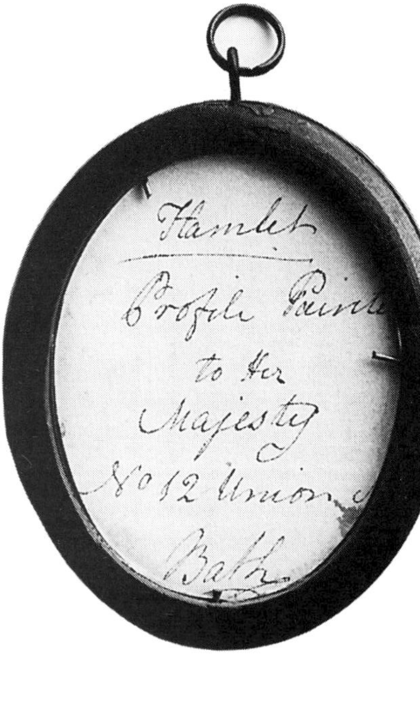

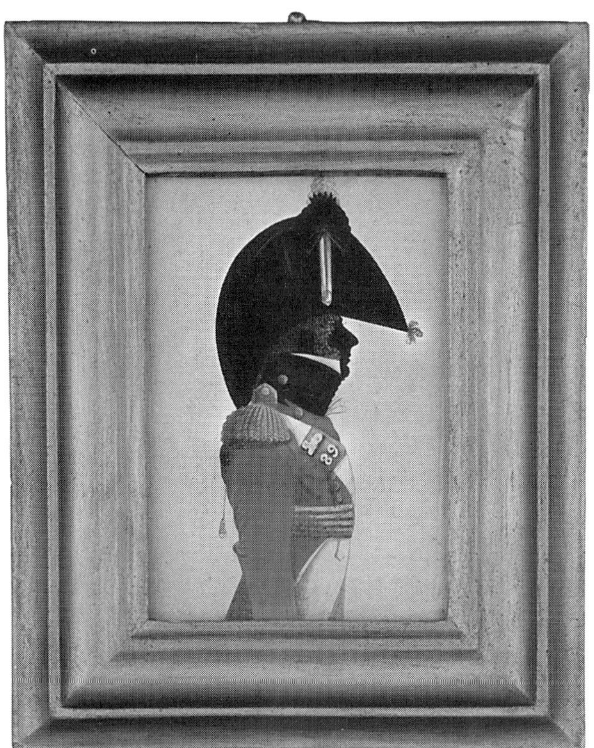

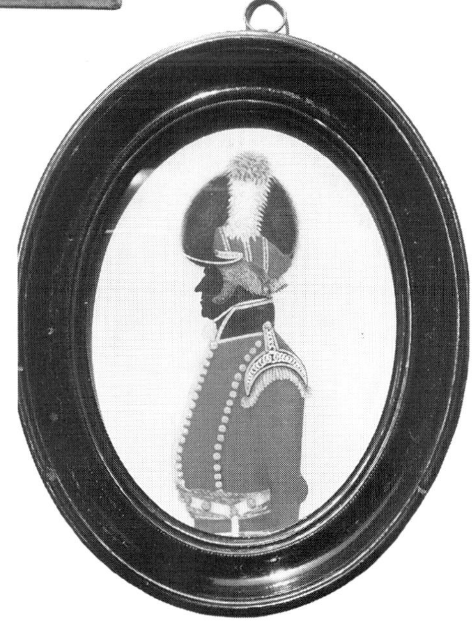

against a red background. Coloured grounds feature only rarely in British silhouette painting, although they are relatively common in Germany, where they are to be found surrounded by painted wreaths or ornamental frames. Spornberg often added the name of the sitter to the base of his works, as was the German custom, but, because he had to write in reverse, some of the letters are occasionally back to front! Most of Spornberg's silhouettes are to be seen in characteristic stamped brass 'Bath' frames.

During the Napoleonic wars Newport, on the Isle of Wight, was a garrison town for the British army. Charles and John Buncombe (*fl. c.*1795-1830) operated a silhouette business almost exclusively devoted to military officers. Their work is not necessarily of the very finest quality,

19

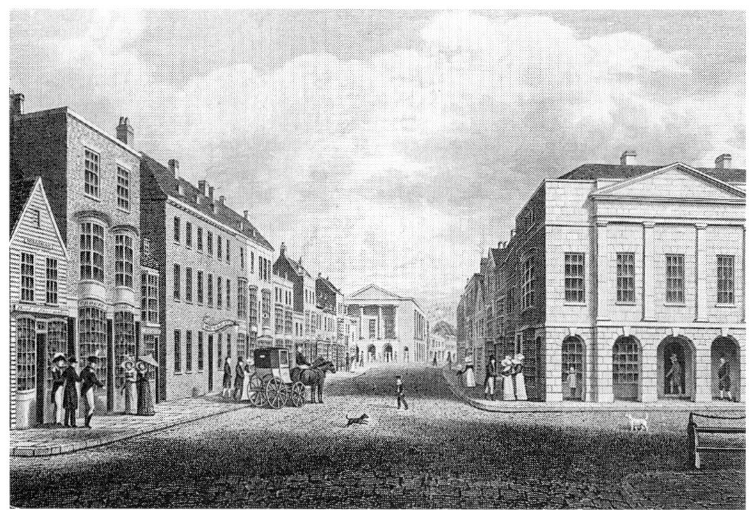

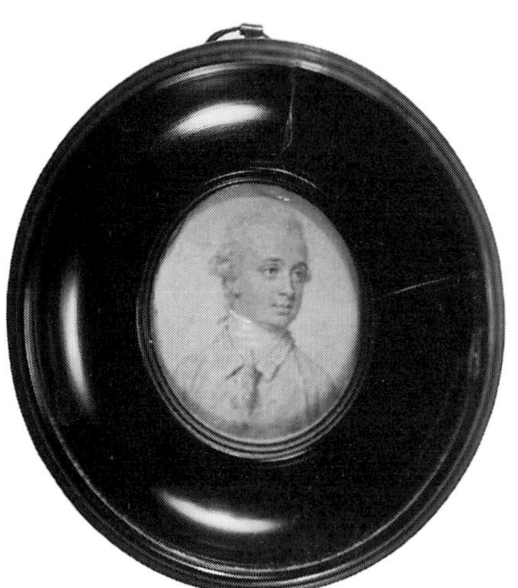

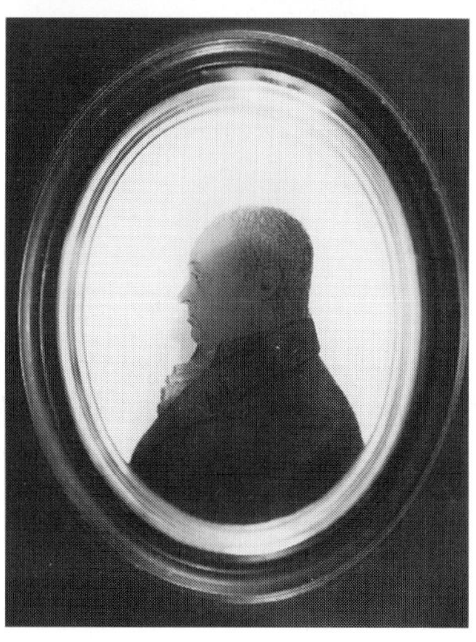

Above left: John Smart, c.1780: John Bullock of the Tower of London. Miniature painted on card. Turned pearwood frame.

Above right: Arthur Lea of Portsmouth, 1809: John Bullock of the Tower of London, aged sixty-three. Silhouette stipple-painted on the reverse of convex glass, backed by a plaster slab. Papier-mâché frame. Although Lea's work is rarely inscribed and never labelled, his unusual technique is easily recognisable. The verre églomisé border is typical of his work.

being rather stiff and literal, but it has always had a definite decorative and romantic attraction. There is an intense poignancy in these brightly painted silhouettes, with their meticulously rendered uniforms, which the officers would proudly post home to their loved ones before embarking for the wars.

20

NINETEENTH-CENTURY SILHOUETTES

The popular success of silhouette painting in the early nineteenth century was partly due to its simple and effective technology, which allowed comparatively unskilled operatives to travel around and provide cheap and lifelike cut images. Profile cutters were very imaginative in inventing names to describe their art: 'Skiagraphy', 'Scissorgraphy', 'Papyrology', 'Papyrolomia' and 'Papyrography' are but a few examples. According to Mrs E. Nevill Jackson, writing in 1911, 'Scissortype' was still being used in Suffolk to describe a silhouette, regardless of what technique was used.

In 1806 Charles Schmalcalder applied for a patent of a more advanced system than Lavater's chair and screen. This apparatus was virtually a machine for making silhouettes, complete with complex screws, clamps and adjustment rods. Under the name of 'Prosopographus, the Automaton Artist', it was transported around Britain by Charles Hervé II during the 1820s. The machine was dressed as a dummy in flowing robes and was worked by a concealed operator. The results, which were then bronzed by hand, were surprisingly good. Another refinement to the system of making silhouettes, incorporating the principles of the sculptor's 'pointing machine', was developed by

Below left: T. London, c.1810: an unknown lady. Silhouette painted on ivory. Papier-mâché frame. Although ivory was the favoured support of miniature painters, it was seldom used by silhouettists, apart from small jewellery work.

Below right: William Alport, c.1806-10: an unknown gentleman. Silhouette painted on card. Papier-mâché frame. The frame hanger is inscribed 'Bullock' but these silhouettes are now known to be the work of Alport, carried out at Bullock's 'Museum of National History and Antiquities' in Liverpool.

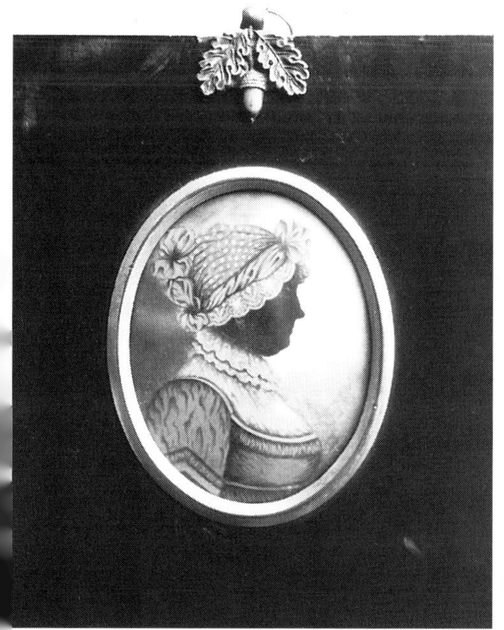

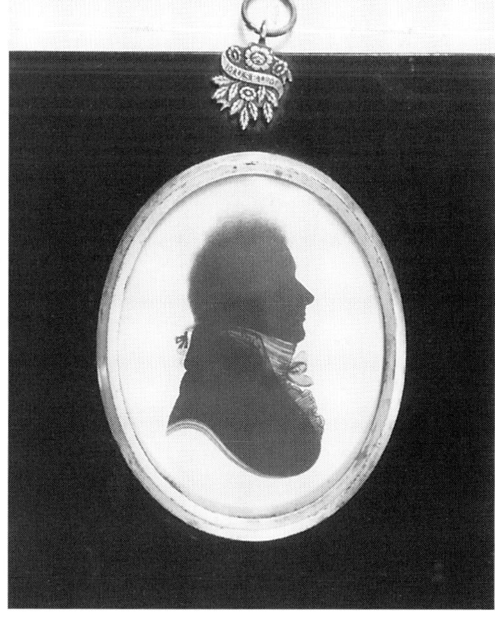

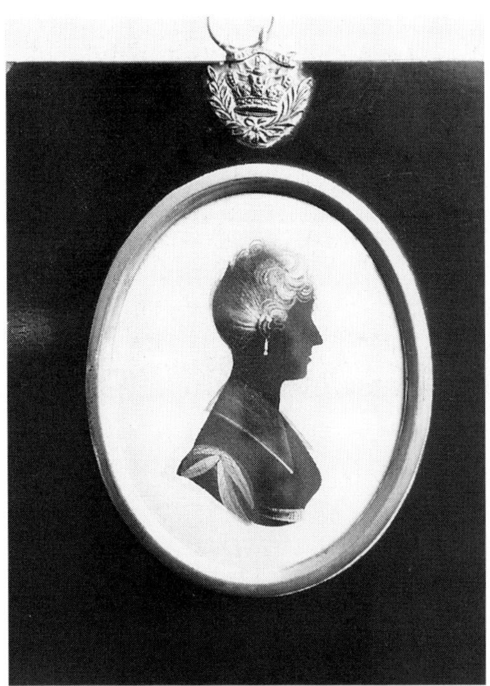 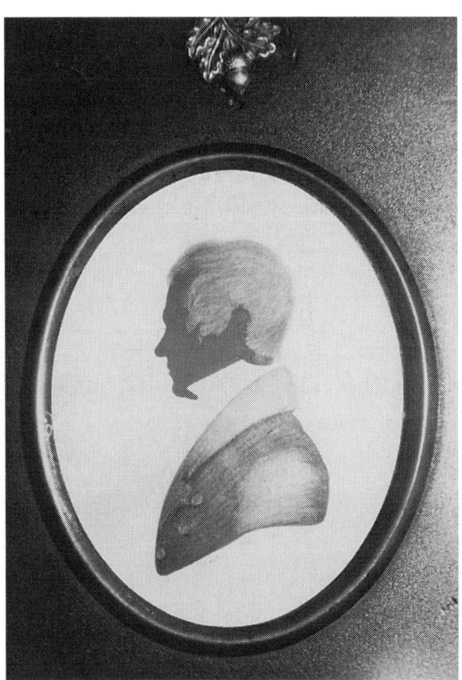

Above left: I. (or J.) Hallam, c.1822: an unknown woman. Silhouette painted on card, in gold and gum arabic against a sepia base colour. Papier-mâché frame with brass hanger showing the artist's name and a royal crown.

Above right: Edward Foster, 1834: an unknown gentleman. Silhouette painted in 'Venetian red' and bronzed. Signed obverse.

Joseph Tussaud, son of the famous wax modeller Marie Tussaud. Joseph and his brother Francis travelled the country with their mother's waxworks; they cut silhouettes with their machine by day and in the evening played in the orchestra or quadrille band! A similar machine was used to great effect by the venerable Edward Foster (1762-1864), the 'Derbyshire Silhouettist and Centenarian'. Hervé, Tussaud and Foster were gifted artists who used these mechanisms to their best advantage. However, they proved the exception rather than the rule, and with the democratisation of silhouettes their overall quality began to decline. In Charles Dickens's *Pickwick Papers*, written in 1836, Sam Weller talks of the 'Profeel Macheen' which creates silhouettes in two and a quarter minutes. This probably represents the lowest point in the aesthetic history of silhouettes.

During the Regency period the focus of elegant attention moved from Bath to Brighton. John Constable, writing in the late 1820s, complained of the artificiality of the resort, calling it 'the receptacle of the fashion and off-scouring of London'. Whilst silhouettists such as George Atkinson (*fl. c.*1806-26) endeavoured to uphold the tradition of silhouette painting, producing good-quality work for a royal and upper-class clientele, the status of the silhouette was beginning to change as the smart, expensive studios of North Parade, Bath, gave way to booths on the newly opened Chain Pier at Brighton. The pier supported two artists, J. Gapp (*fl.*

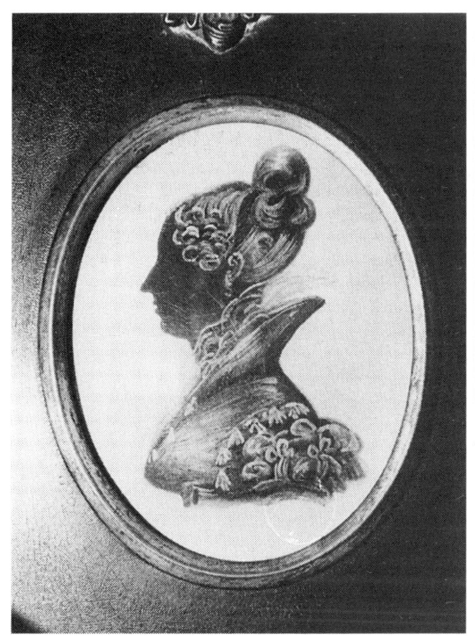

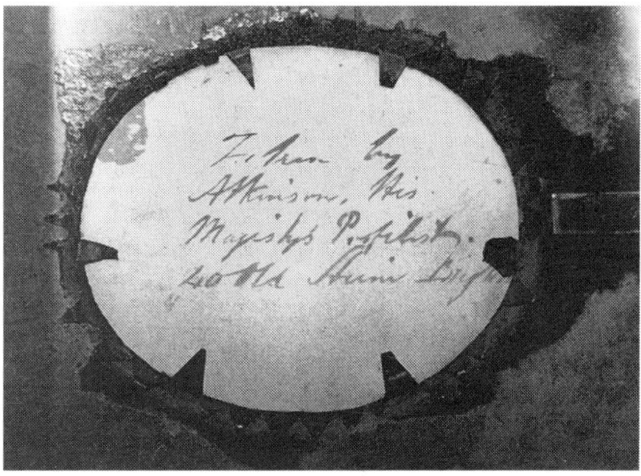

Above: George Atkinson: trade label number 1: 'Taken by Atkinson, His Majesty's Profilist. 40 Old Steine Brighton.'

Left: George Atkinson, c.1820: an unknown lady. Silhouette painted on card, in gold against a black background. Trade label number 1. Papier-mâché frame.

Below: The Chain Pier, Brighton, in 1842. The first of all the promenade piers, it was built in 1823 and destroyed by a storm in 1896. Two silhouettists were installed on the pier during this period: J. Gapp, 'the original Profilist for cutting accurate Likenesses, attends Daily at the Third Tower in the centre'; and his rival, Edward Haines, who seems to have occupied different towers at different times.

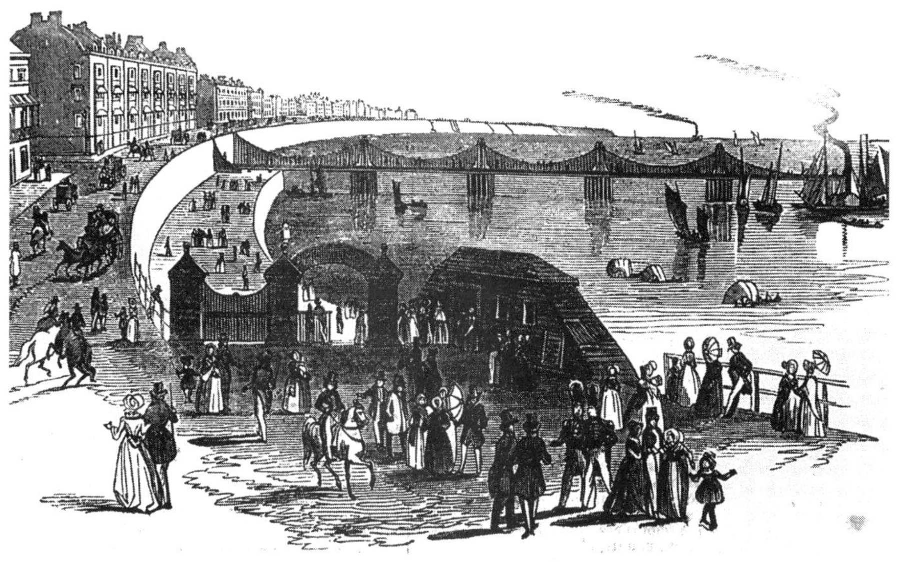

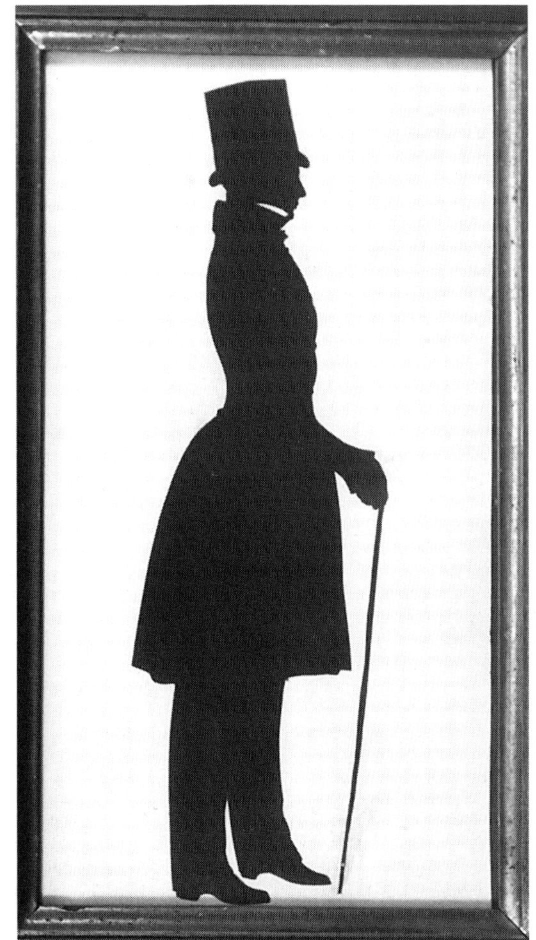

Left: J. Gapp, c.1840: an unknown gentleman. Cut silhouette. The subject wears the 'Wellington' top hat fashionable in the late 1830s.

Right: Augustin Edouart, 1830: Master John Brown Innes presenting a rose to Mrs Sutherland; Jane and Rachel Anderson playing with a dog. Double-sided cut-out on card, inscribed with the sitters' details and dated 1830. This, and the two group silhouettes on the next page, come from Edouart's copybooks, retrieved from the wreck of the 'Oneida'.

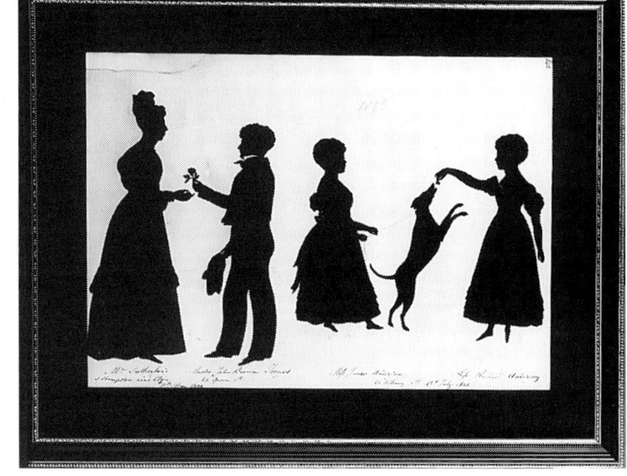

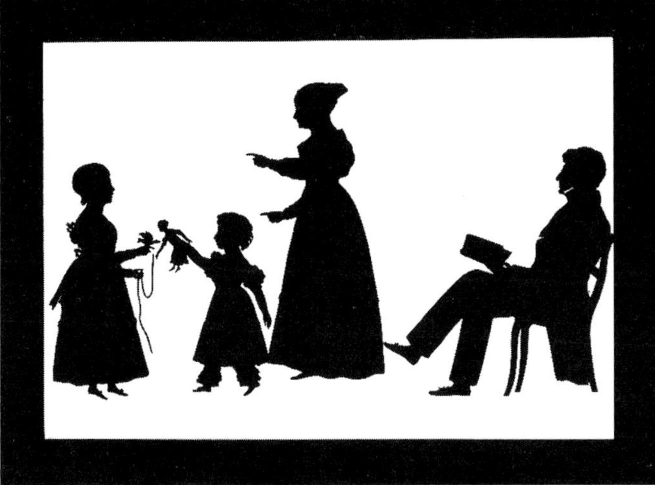

Augustin Edouart, 1831: Miss Maria Gibson holding a doll; Mr and Mrs Archibald Gibson. Double-sided cut-out on card, inscribed with the sitters' details and dated 1831.

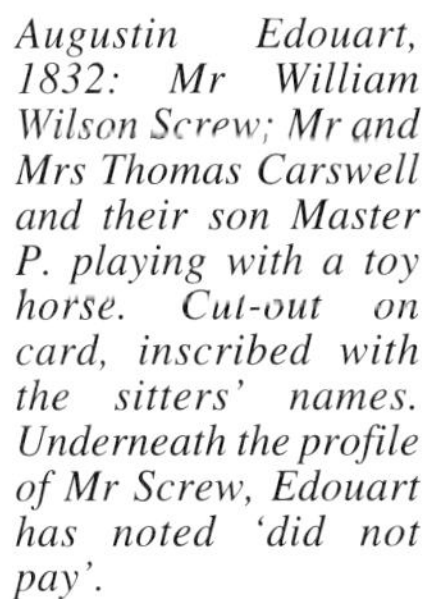

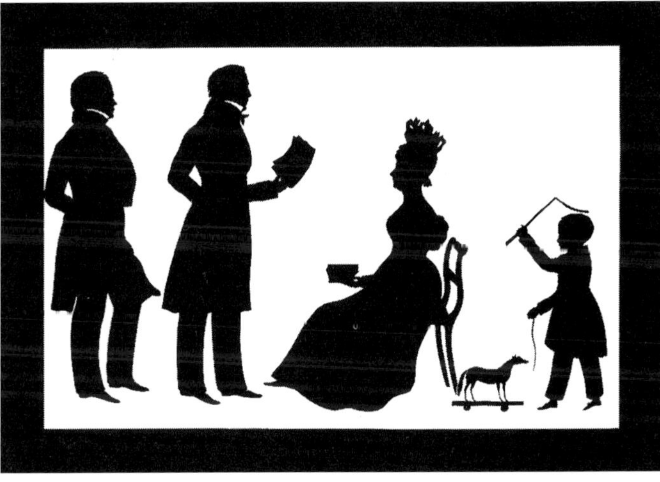

Augustin Edouart, 1832: Mr William Wilson Screw; Mr and Mrs Thomas Carswell and their son Master P. playing with a toy horse. Cut-out on card, inscribed with the sitters' names. Underneath the profile of Mr Screw, Edouart has noted 'did not pay'.

1827-40), who had a booth 'at the Third Tower in the centre', and E. Haines (*fl. c.*1827-96), at 'the first left-hand tower', who described himself as a 'Profilist and Scissorgraphist'. Both of these prolific artists produced simple, rapidly cut full-length silhouettes. They supplemented their income by producing small cut silhouettes as souvenirs to be stuck in ladies' scrapbooks or framed in cheap stained-deal surrounds.

The decline of the silhouette as an art form was arrested by Augustin Edouart (1789-1861). Edouart was born in Dunkerque, served in the Napoleonic wars and, at the age of nineteen, managed a china factory. He came to England in 1814 and made a living selling fancy pictures and copies of prints made out of human hair. Edouart declared that he took up silhouette painting as a form of therapy to ward off the depression caused by the death of his wife in 1825, but he was also a shrewd businessman and probably saw the financial possibilities of well-produced silhouettes. At this stage he was unaware of great earlier artists such as Miers, Mrs Beetham and Rosenberg and had seen only the work of weak mechanical 'pier-head' cutters. Although the word 'silhouette' was coined in France in the eighteenth century, it is due to Edouart that it has

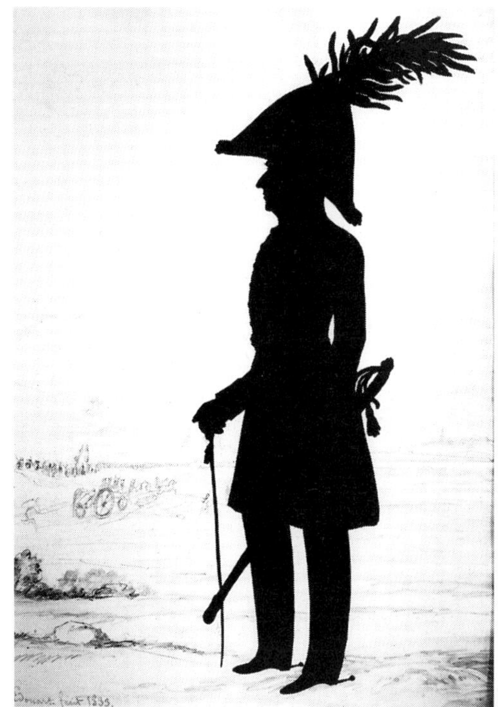

Above: Augustin Edouart, 1833: Colonel Robert Samuel Hustler. Silhouette cut-out on card with a battle scene in the background.

entered the English language. When he first used the word in advertising his work, the public were disappointed that 'silhouette' meant simply 'black shade', which they were already accustomed to.

Edouart's treatise *Silhouette Likenesses*, published in 1835, was an attempt to raise the status of an art that had lost direction. In it he bemoans the childish bad taste of the public, citing in particular the vogue for the bronzing of hair and the various coloured embellishments of the dress: 'Is it not ridiculous to see such harlequinades? The face, being quite black, forms such a contrast that everyone looks like a negro.' It is unclear which particular artists Edouart was objecting to, for very few worked in colour to any great extent. However, possible candidates might be John Dempsey (*fl. c.*1830-45) or W. H. Beaumont (*fl. c.*1830-50).

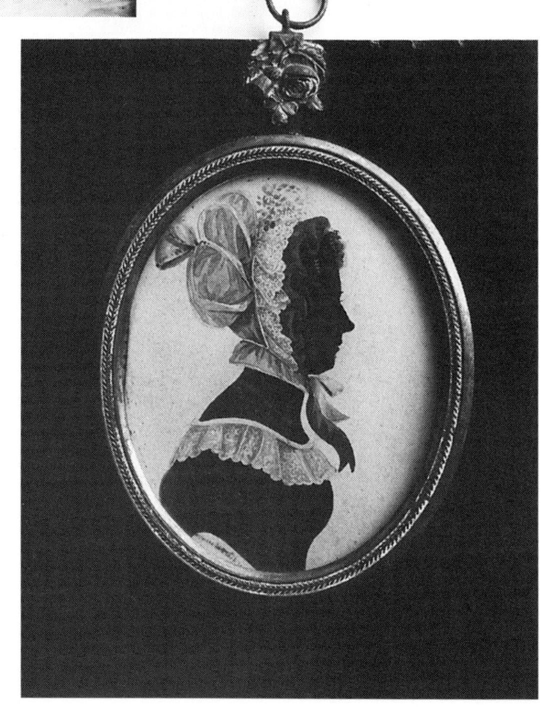

Right: M. H. Frost, c.1830: an unknown lady. Silhouette painted on paper with detail in colour. Papiermâché frame. The sitter wears a red coral necklace, which is the type of embellishment that Edouart objected to in his book 'Silhouette Likenesses', published in 1835.

Edouart expresses in his treatise the idea that the attitude and demeanour of the sitter are just as important as the contours of the face in expressing character. The grouping together of figures has the effect of emphasising likeness by making features such as height, gesture or attitude more apparent. Edouart also stresses that the sitter should wear his usual dress to provide further characterisation. There is nothing particularly radical in these ideas and much of what he wrote would

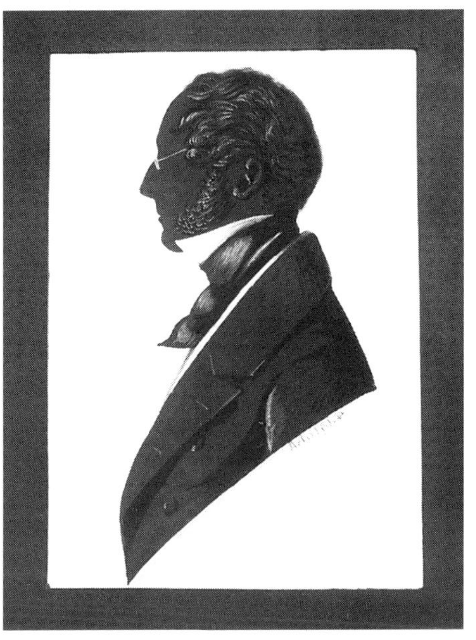

Right: 'Monsieur' Edgar Adolphe, c.1840: P. Carthew Esquire. Silhouette painted on card with detail in gum arabic and gold. From an album.

Below left: Samuel Metford, c.1840: an unknown lady. Cut silhouette with lithographed background. A sea view seen through a window is typical of Metford's work. Notice how the room setting is a continuation of the room in the next illustration.

Below right: Samuel Metford, c.1840: an unknown lady. Cut silhouette with lithographed background.

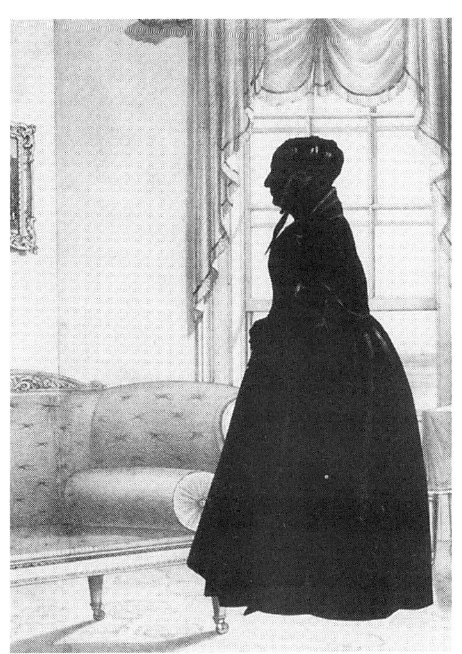

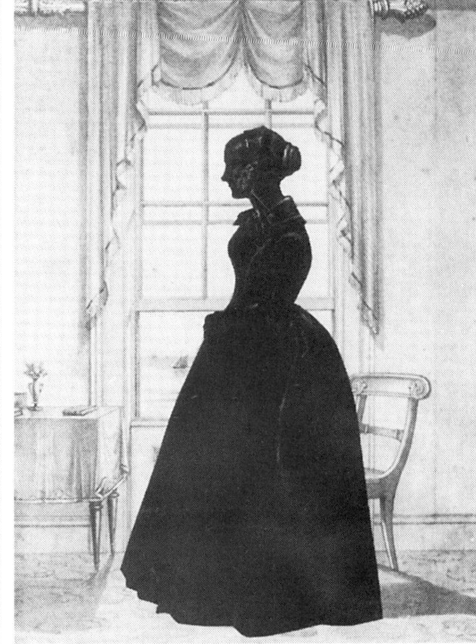

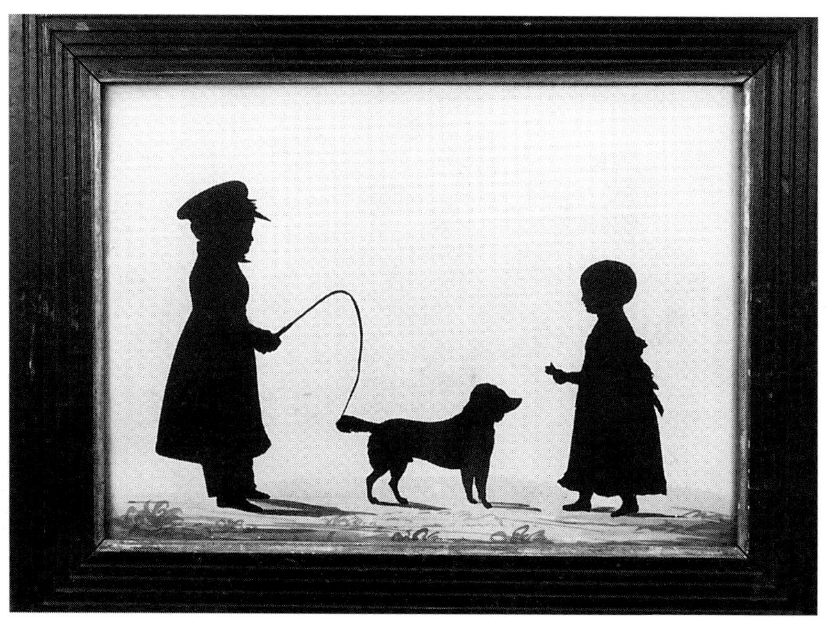

W. J. Hubard: 'Robert Warren aged 4 and Gracie Warren aged 2. 1824.' Cut-out group silhouette. Trade label number 3. 'Cut with common Scissors, By that singularly gifted Little Boy, Master Hubard, Without Drawing or Machine.'

have been apparent to any art student trained at the Royal Academy Schools. Nevertheless, this is a unique book in that it represents the only systematic analysis of the silhouette maker's art of the nineteenth century.

Edouart was an extraordinarily prolific artist and seems to have cut freehand more than one hundred thousand silhouettes. These were mostly full-length in format and included groups and genre scenes often set against a lithographed background. Practically every silhouette was signed and most were framed in bird's-eye maple frames supplied by the artist. Edouart kept duplicates of all his work carefully annotated and indexed in large folios. Tragically, on his way home from America, the ship *Oneida* was wrecked off Guernsey and out of a hundred thousand silhouettes only some twelve thousand were ever recovered. This experience proved so profoundly depressing that Edouart never cut another silhouette and a short time later, in 1861, he died in Calais. On seeing a collection of Edouart's work in Paris, Charlie Chaplin exclaimed: 'This is the ancestor of cinema.'

Several other nineteenth-century artists are worthy of mention. William Hubard (1807-62) was a boy prodigy who cut his first silhouette at the age of twelve. After touring Britain as 'The Hubard Gallery' for fourteen years, he emigrated to America and eventually became a successful portrait painter. His silhouettes tend to be slightly coarse in their cutting and bronzing but 'Master Hubard' enjoyed a celebrity status for his precocity. Not much is known about the prolific Frederick and Henry Albert Frith, known as the 'Royal Victoria Gallery'. They produced fine full-length and group silhouettes with attractive bronzing in the 1840s and 1850s. Virtually disregarded at the beginning of the twentieth century, their inventive silhouettes will stand comparison with some of the best Georgian examples and now enjoy the rightful attention of collectors.

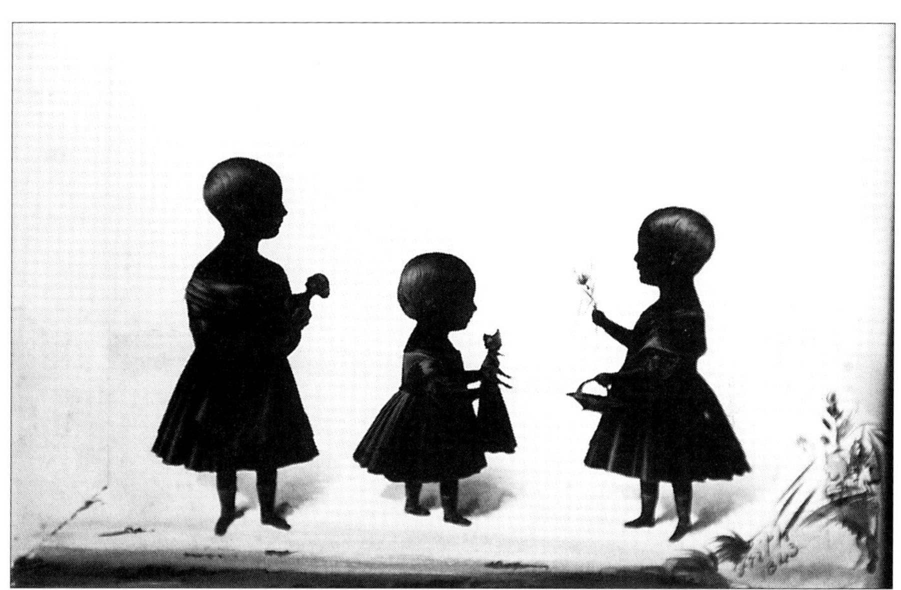

Royal Victoria Gallery, 1844: unknown children. Cut silhouette with detail in gold, signed 'Frith' and dated 1844. Probably by Henry Albert Frith.

Royal Victoria Gallery, 1844: an unknown boy riding a horse and a girl holding a riding crop. Cut silhouette with detail in gold, signed 'Frith' and dated 1844.

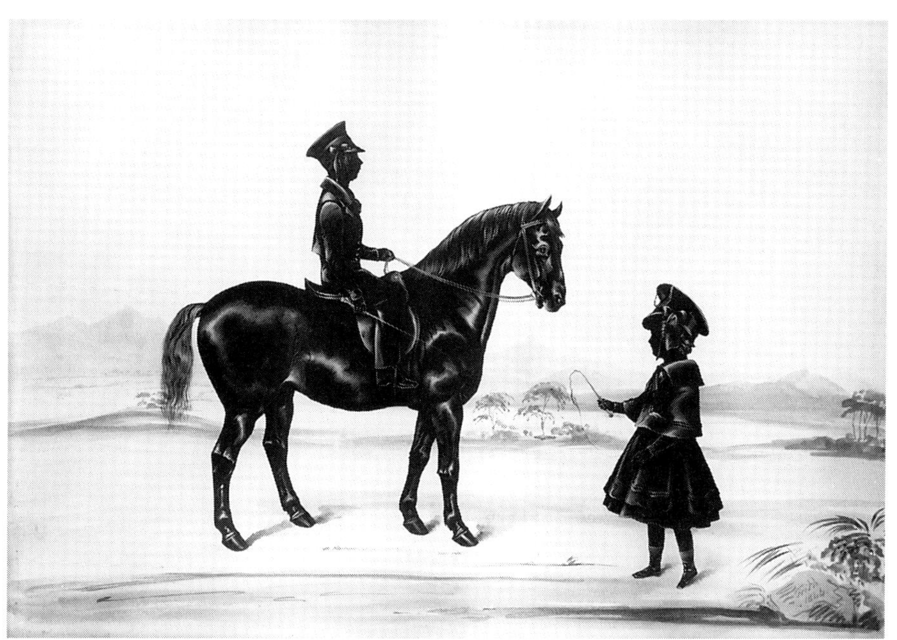

COLLECTING SILHOUETTES

The factors governing the collectability of particular silhouettes include artistic quality, rarity, historical interest, condition, originality and the presence of trade labels. Because silhouettists only rarely signed their work, trade labels assume an important role. All other considerations being equal, a beautiful Georgian lady or a dashing military officer are generally more desirable than an overweight clergyman. Chipped or cracked plaster, peeling wax backings, heavy discolouration, replaced frames and missing trade labels have a negative effect on the desirability of silhouettes. Whilst silhouettes by the leading artists in good condition with unbroken trade labels are likely to be expensive, many silhouettes can still be bought for little more than the net worth of their frames.

It should be remembered that it used to be common practice to commission copies of cherished silhouettes, often quite a few years later, by the original artist or others. In these cases, the trade label is likely to be a more reliable guide to the date than the costume. More seriously in terms of value, as in all fields of collecting, one occasionally encounters fakes. Beware especially of fake military Buncombes; because of their decorative value and ease of copying, they have provided profitable employment for fakers over the years.

Silhouettes were not necessarily intended to be framed and hung on the wall, as some were made for albums, but when they are framed the frame adds another dimension to the work. Reframing not only

J. H. Gillespie, c.1815: silhouette painted in sepia. (Left) Acidity in the paper has led to a pronounced 'browning', and the sepia ink and gum arabic have attracted mould. (Right) The same silhouette after expert restoration.

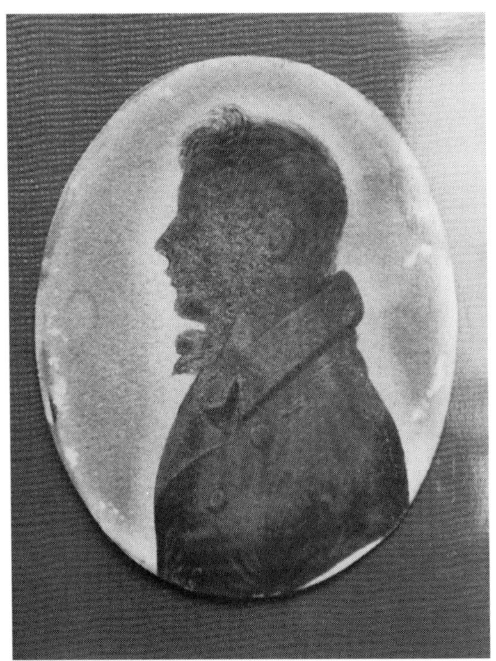 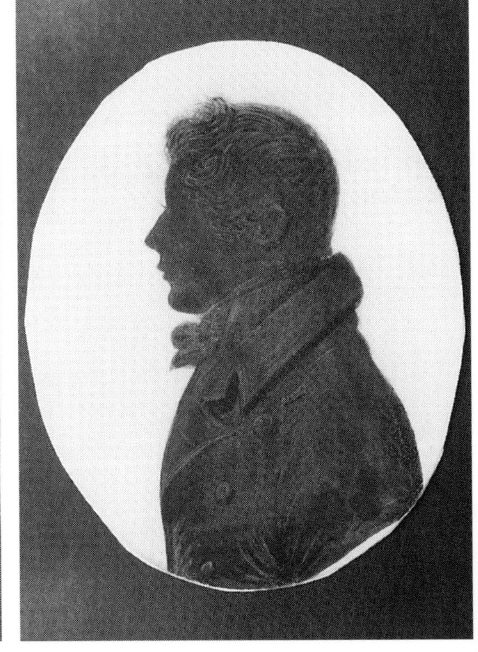

affects the aesthetic harmony of the whole but often leads to the loss of important historical information in the form of inscriptions and trade labels. The breaking of a trade label to remove the silhouette from its frame should be avoided at all costs.

Many of the earliest silhouettists, such as Sarah Harrington, used delicately turned oval pearwood frames stained to imitate ebony. These tend to split with the passage of time as a result of shrinkage across the grain. Stamped brass oval frames with gadrooned borders were often used in the 1790s. Certain artists favoured particular forms of frame. Much of Jacob Spornberg's work is to be seen in rectangular stamped brass frames with gadrooned borders and a built-in spandrel mount. In form, these are miniature versions of the gilt wood print frames of the period.

The earliest forms of the characteristic rectangular papier-mâché lacquered frame start to appear at the very end of the eighteenth century. They differ from the nineteenth-century versions in several respects: they retain a turned pearwood bezel for holding the steeply domed glass in place and have a simple brass suspension ring instead of elaborately patterned hangers. Lea of Portsmouth often used this type of frame. With the nineteenth century came the mass production of lacquer papier-mâché frames, which are often to be found stamped with the maker's name, such as Clay or Hill of Birmingham. The bezels and hangers are of stamped, lacquered brass in various patterns – starburst, baskets of flowers and acorns amongst others.

In the Victorian period half-length and full-length silhouettes that necessitated larger frames proliferated. Typically, these frames were veneered in rosewood or bird's-eye maple with a gilt wood fillet and are identical to the print frames of the period. Cheaper, more primitive silhouettes were often framed in channel-moulded stained deal frames.

FURTHER READING

Cunnington, C. Willett and Phillis. *Handbook of English Costume in the Eighteenth Century*. Faber & Faber, 1972.

Hickman, Peggy. *Two Centuries of Silhouettes. Celebrities in Profile*. A. & C. Black, 1971.

Hickman, Peggy. *Silhouettes* (exhibition catalogue). National Portrait Gallery, London, 1972.

Jackson, E. Nevill. *The History of Silhouettes*. Connoisseur, 1911.

Jackson, E. Nevill. *Silhouette. Notes and Dictionary*. Methuen, 1938.

McKechnie, Sue. *British Silhouette Artists and Their Work 1760-1860*. Sotheby Parke Bernet, 1978.

Mayne, Arthur. 'Profile Miniatures in the V. & A., Part II, The Pollak Collection', *The Antique Collector*, February 1966.

Mayne, Arthur. *British Profile Miniaturists*. Faber & Faber, 1970.

Pollak, Jack. 'Identifying English Silhouettes', *The Antique Collector*, November-December 1948.

Pollak, Jack. 'Profile Art in Decadence 1830-1850?', *The Antique Collector*, October 1955.

Pollak, Jack. 'The Silhouette on Jewellery and China', *The Antique Collector*, May 1978.

PLACES TO VISIT

Museum displays may be altered and readers are advised to telephone before visiting to check that relevant items are on show, as well as to find out opening times.

Brighton Museum and Art Gallery, 4-5 Pavilion Buildings, Brighton BN1 1EE. Telephone: 01273 603005.

Bristol City Museum and Art Gallery, Queen's Road, Bristol BS8 1RL. Telephone: 0117-922 3571.

British Museum, Great Russell Street, London WC1B 3DG. Telephone: 0171-636 1555.

Holburne Museum and Crafts Study Centre, Great Pulteney Street, Bath BA2 4DB. Telephone: 01225 466669.

Killerton House, Broadclyst, near Exeter EX5 3LE. Telephone: 01392 881345. (National Trust.)

National Portrait Gallery, St Martin's Place, London WC2H 0HE. Telephone: 0171-306 0055.

Victoria and Albert Museum, Cromwell Road, South Kensington, London SW7 2RL. Telephone: 0171-938 8500.

Victoria Art Gallery, Bridge Street, Bath BA2 4AT. Telephone: 01225 477772.

ACKNOWLEDGEMENTS
The author gratefully acknowledges the help received from Diana Joll, Secretary of the Silhouette Collectors' Club, and Harold Ward for allowing me to photograph their collections; Emma Rutherford and Sarah Allen of Bonhams, for helping me to procure photographs from the Christie and Pollak collections, and Bonhams for allowing me to reproduce them. Sonia Cashman, Cynthia Walmsley and Pixie Taylor kindly allowed me to photograph their silhouettes. My thanks also to Caroline Joss and Richard Ratcliffe for their helpful advice. Illustrations are acknowledged as follows: Bonhams, pages 1, 4, 5 (top), 13, 16, 18 (top), 19 (top), 24 (bottom), 25 (both), 26 (top), 29 (bottom), also cover (top right and centre); Sonia Cashman, page 17 (both); Diana Joll, pages 2, 6, 7, 8 (both), 9 (all), 11 (top), 12, 18 (lower two), 21 (left), 26 (bottom), 27 (top), 29 (top), also cover (top left); Pixie Taylor, page 14 (bottom); Cynthia Walmsley, page 14 (top); Harold Ward, pages 5 (bottom), 20 (lower two), 21 (right), 22 (left), 24 (top), 27 (lower two), 28; the author, pages 10, 11 (bottom), 15, 19 (bottom), 20 (top), 22 (right), 23 (all), 30 (both), also cover (lower).